My First Book about the Alphabet of Rabbits & Hares

Amazing Animal Books Children's Picture Books

By Molly Davidson

Mendon Cottage Books

JD-Biz Publishing

Read More Amazing Animal Books

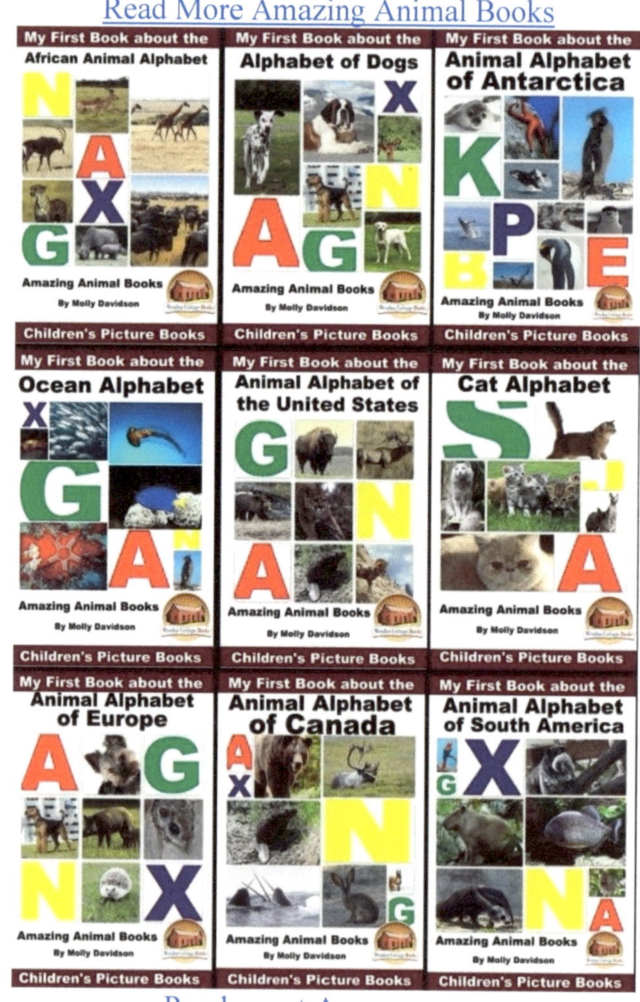

Purchase at Amazon.com

Download Free Books!

http://MendonCottageBooks.com

Introduction

There are a few differences between rabbits and hares, the first being hares have longer back legs than rabbits.

Second, rabbits stay the same color all year round and hares are dark in the summer and white in the winter.

 is for an Arctic Hare.

The arctic hare is the largest of all hare species, weighing up to 15 pounds.

Their white fur provides camouflage against the white snow and ice of the tundra where they live.

 **is for a Belgian Hare.**

Belgian hares are a fancy breed of pet rabbit, originally bred in Belgium, in 1888.

It is one of the most intelligent and energetic rabbits.

C is for a California Rabbit.

California rabbits have between 8 - 12 babies (called kits) at a time.

They make great pets, due to their kind and easy going personalities.

D is for a Dice's Cottontail.

Dice's cottontails live in the forests of Panama and Costa Rica.

Like most rabbits and hares they eat their own poop, it is easier to digest.

 is for an European Rabbit.

When they are not eating they are digging borrows, which are tunnels that run underground, also called warrens.

European rabbits can up to 7 liters (groups) of 2 - 12 babies per year!

 is for a French Lop.

French lop rabbits have long ears that can grow as long as 8 inches.

All rabbits are very social animals, and if kept as a pet, they should have at least one other rabbit for company.

G is for a Granada Hare.

Juan Lacruz © **Wikimedia Commons**

The Granada hare is also known as the Iberian hare, since it lives on the Iberian Peninsula, on the south west corner of Europe.

They will jump up in the air and twist in order to attract a mate.

 is for a Holland Lop.

Holland lop rabbits enjoy eating lettuce, spinach, parsley, dill, coriander, endive, fennel, arugula, and carrots.

They were first bred in the Netherlands.

I is for an Indian Hare.

N. A. Naseer © <u>Wikimedia Commons</u>

The Indian hare is also known as the black naped hare, due to its black neck.

They live on the many islands surrounding the Indian subcontinent.

J is for a Japanese Hare.

Alpsdake © <u>Wikimedia Commons</u>

Japanese hare males (boys) will stand on their back legs and box each other in order to keep the female (girl) safe and all to themselves.

K is for Koslov's Pika.

Pika's are cousins to the rabbits; they have much shorter ears.

Koslov's pika lives only in the tundra of China and is on the endangered list.

L is for a Lionhead Rabbit.

Lionhead rabbits get their name because they have a mane of fur surrounding their face, making them look like a lion.

They are small pet rabbits, weighing no more than 3 3/4 pounds.

M is for a **Mountain Cottontail.**

They live primarily in the Rocky Mountains and Cascade-Sierra Nevada Mountains of the United States and Canada.

They have hair that covers the feet for warmth.

 is for a Netherland Dwarf Rabbit.

Netherland dwarf rabbits are very small, weighing less than 2 1/2 pounds.

They are poplar as show rabbits because of their baby looking faces and small size.

O is for an Omilteme Cottontail.

The omilteme cottontail is one of the most endangered rabbit species in the World.

They can be found only in the mountains of Guerrero, Mexico.

P is for a Polish Rabbit.

Eponimm © **Wikimedia Commons**

Even though it is named the Polish rabbit, it was actually started in England.

They don't like hot temperatures, and do well in cold temperatures, as long as they are kept dry.

Q is for Halequin Rabbit.

EQUINOXE79 @ Wikimedia Commons

They are very intelligent and playful rabbits.

Halequin rabbits can be trained to use a litter box and respond to its own name.

R is for a Riverine Rabbit.

They're the most endangered mammals in the World, with only about 250 adults alive today.

They are only found in the Karoo Desert of South Africa.

S is for a Snowshoe Hare.

They have large feet which help them hop across the snow, instead of falling through.

A snowshoe hare will only live for about 1 year in the wild.

Their fur is brown in the summer and turns white for camouflage in the winter.

S is also for a Swamp Rabbit.

glenn_e_wilson © **Wikimedia Commons**

Swamp rabbits are a large cottontail that lives in the swamps of the southern United States.

They will swim to escape predators and hide under brush or other water plants with only their nose out of the water.

T is for a Tolai Hare.

Tolai hares are mainly nocturnal, which means active at night.

They are a very common hare found living in the deserts throughout most of central Asia.

 is for a Velveteen Lop.

The fictional character the velveteen rabbit is based off this lop eared rabbit.

They have very soft fur and love to be held and cuddled.

 **is for a White-Tailed Jackrabbit.**

White-tailed jackrabbits sleep for most of the day in a small hole under a bush; they wake up at dusk ready to eat.

They can run as fast as 34 mph and leap as far as 16 feet per bounce.

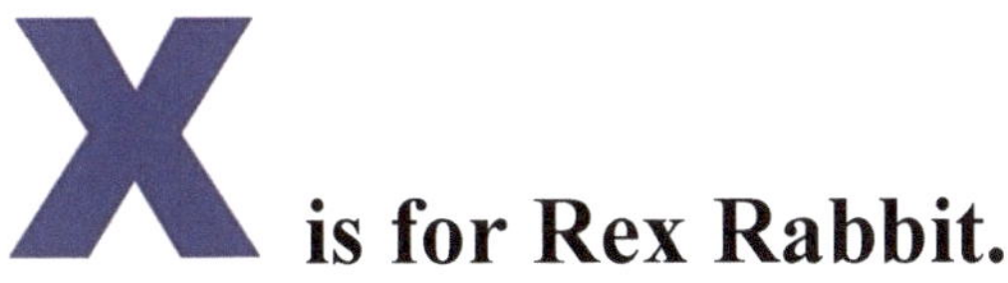 **X** is for Rex Rabbit.

Rex rabbits have very plush, velvety fur.

Does (girls) have a dewlap, which is a large flap of skin under the chin.

 is for a Yunnan Hare.

Daderot @ **Wikimedia Commons**

They are found living in China in the province of Yunnan.

The biggest a Yunnan hare will get it 18 inches long and about 5 1/2 pounds.

Z is for a Zacatuche.

dispale © **Wikimedia Commons**

Zacatuche are also called volcano rabbits and are only found in the mountains of Mexico.

They make a high-pitched sound to warn other rabbits of danger.

Conclusion

Rabbits are one of the top 5 most popular pets in the United States.

If you would like one, do plenty of research to find the right fit for you and your family.

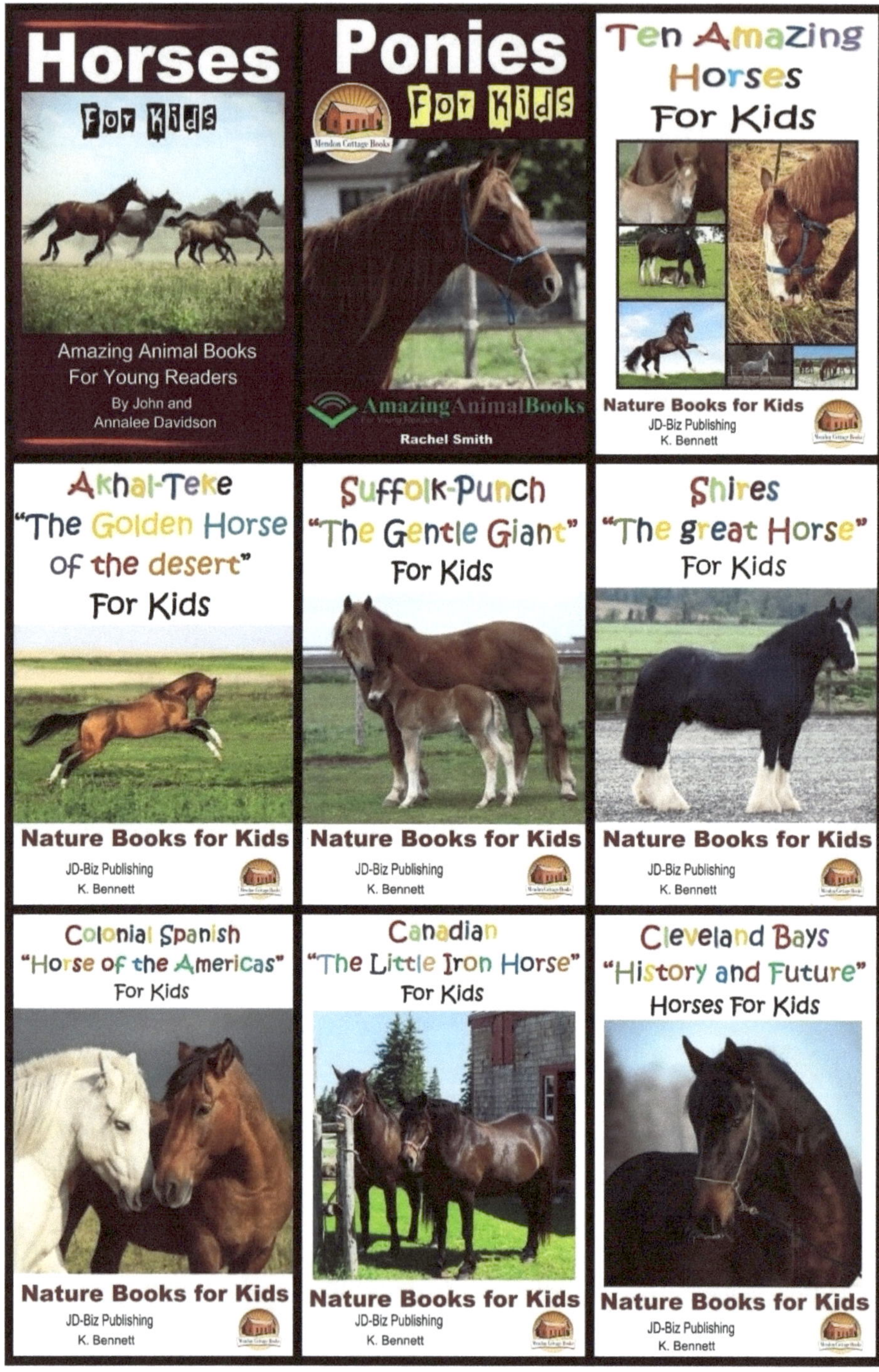

Horses
For Kids
Amazing Animal Books
For Young Readers
By John and
Annalee Davidson

Ponies
For Kids
Mendon Cottage Books
Amazing Animal Books
For Young Readers
Rachel Smith

Ten Amazing
Horses
For Kids
Nature Books for Kids
JD-Biz Publishing
K. Bennett

Akhal-Teke
"The Golden Horse
of the desert"
For Kids
Nature Books for Kids
JD-Biz Publishing
K. Bennett

Suffolk-Punch
"The Gentle Giant"
For Kids
Nature Books for Kids
JD-Biz Publishing
K. Bennett

Shires
"The great Horse"
For Kids
Nature Books for Kids
JD-Biz Publishing
K. Bennett

Colonial Spanish
"Horse of the Americas"
For Kids
Nature Books for Kids
JD-Biz Publishing
K. Bennett

Canadian
"The Little Iron Horse"
For Kids
Nature Books for Kids
JD-Biz Publishing
K. Bennett

Cleveland Bays
"History and Future"
Horses For Kids
Nature Books for Kids
JD-Biz Publishing
K. Bennett

Top Ten Dog Breeds For Kids
Amazing Animal Books
For Young Readers
Kisha Bennett & John Davidson
German Shepherds
Dog Books for Kids
K. Bennett
Bulldogs
Dog Books for Kids
K. Bennett
Dachshund
Dog Books for Kids
K. Bennett
Poodles
Dog Books for Kids
K. Bennett
Labrador Retrievers
Dog Books for Kids
K. Bennett
Rottweilers
Dog Books for Kids
K. Bennett
Boxers
Dog Books for Kids
K. Bennett
Golden Retrievers
Dog Books for Kids
K. Bennett
Puppies
Dog Books For Kids
Amazing Animal Books
By John Davidson
Beagles
Dog Books for Kids
K. Bennett
Yorkshire Terriers
Dog Books for Kids
K. Bennett
Dogs
Top Ten Dog Breeds For Kids
Amazing Animal Books
For Young Readers
Zahra Jazeel & John Davidson
Cats
For Kids
Amazing Animal Books
For Young Sheaders
K. Bennett & John Davidson
Foxes
For Kids
Amazing Animal Books
For Young Readers
Zahra Jazeel & John Davidson
Wolves
For Kids
Amazing Animal Books
For Young Readers
By John Davidson and Virginia Fidler

Publisher

JD-Biz Corp

P O Box 374

Mendon, Utah 84325

http://www.jd-biz.com/